PULP

AN ILLUSTRATED BIOGRAPHY BY LINDA HOLORNY

be returned on or before

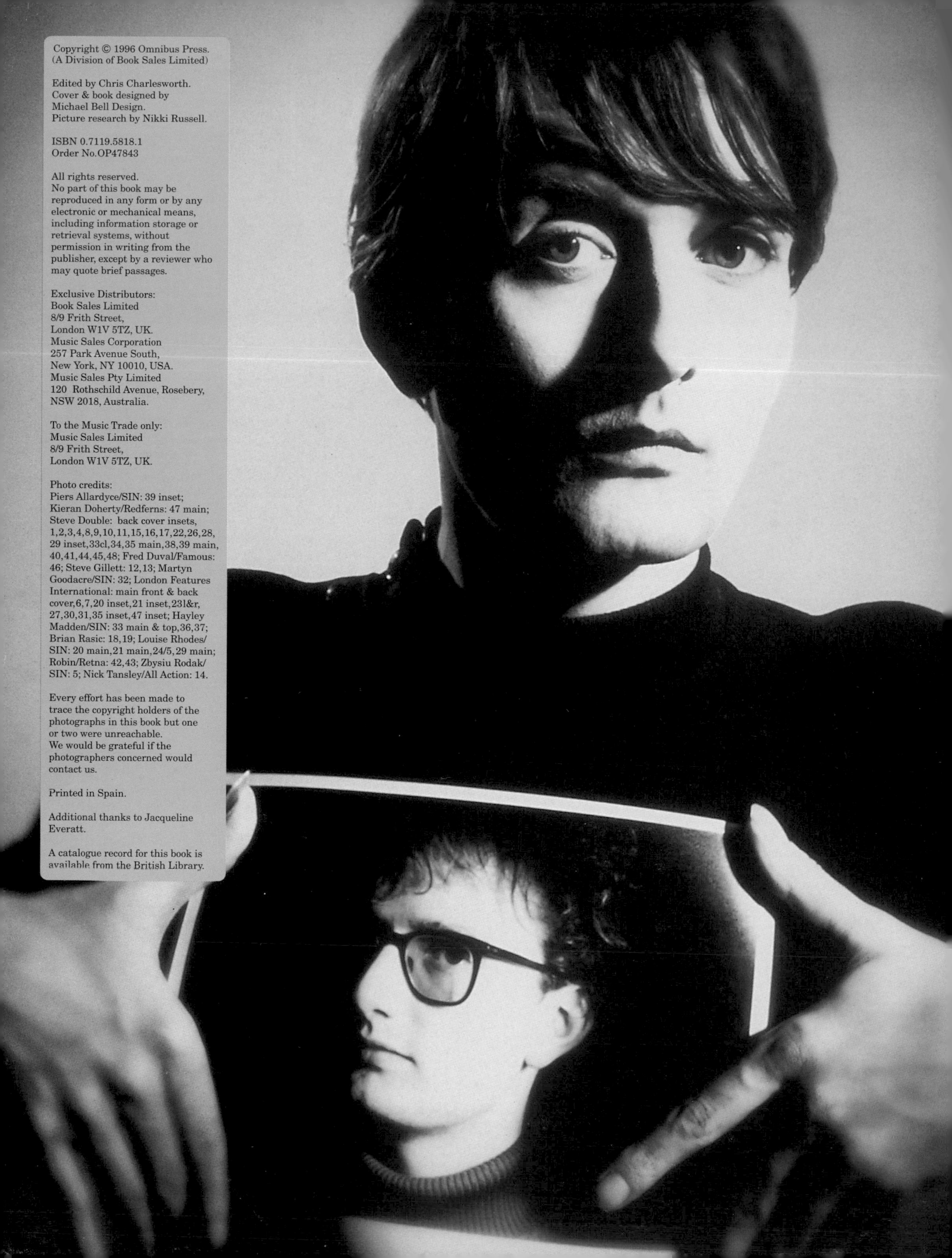

Edited by Chris Charlesworth.
Cover & book designed by
Michael Bell Design.
Picture research by Nikki Russell.

ISBN 0.7119.5818.1
Order No.OP47843

Exclusive Distributors:
Book Sales Limited
8/9 Frith Street,
London W1V 5TZ, UK.
Music Sales Corporation
257 Park Avenue South,
New York, NY 10010, USA.
Music Sales Pty Limited
120 Rothschild Avenue, Rosebery,
NSW 2018, Australia.

To the Music Trade only:
Music Sales Limited
8/9 Frith Street,
London W1V 5TZ, UK.

Photo credits:
Piers Allardyce/SIN: 39 inset; Kieran Doherty/Redferns: 47 main; Steve Double: back cover insets, 1,2,3,4,8,9,10,11,15,16,17,22,26,28, 29 inset,33cl,34,35 main,38,39 main, 40,41,44,45,48; Fred Duval/Famous: 46; Steve Gillett: 12,13; Martyn Goodacre/SIN: 32; London Features International: main front & back cover,6,7,20 inset,21 inset,23l&r, 27,30,31,35 inset,47 inset; Hayley Madden/SIN: 33 main & top,36,37; Brian Rasic: 18,19; Louise Rhodes/ SIN: 20 main,21 main,24/5,29 main; Robin/Retna: 42,43; Zbysiu Rodak/ SIN: 5; Nick Tansley/All Action: 14.

Every effort has been made to trace the copyright holders of the photographs in this book but one or two were unreachable. We would be grateful if the photographers concerned would contact us.

Printed in Spain.

Additional thanks to Jacqueline Everatt.

A catalogue record for this book is available from the British Library.

Pulp. Glam, kitsch, ironic, wacky, honest, patient, deadpan, comical. Space 1999, jumbo collars, brown charity jumble clothes, Raleigh chopper bikes, and council estate sex in Sheffield.

Now let's get this straight – Pulp are none of the above. Pulp are nasty, subversive, scary, sexually deviant, obsessive, peculiar, vindictive and vicious. To have Jarvis Cocker standing in front of 100,000 kids, moulding them in between his elongated thumb and index finger is not pop. At least, not in the sense of Kylie Minogue and bubblegum. It is foul and unclean pop, played out through a collection of filthy mass appeal operas. Jarvis Cocker could even be the anti-Christ of Pop.

Except that is, for Robson & Jerome. 1995 was a great year for music in many ways, Britpop, Glastonbury's 25th, Blur vs Oasis, no Sting album. But where there is light there is dark. And Robson & Jerome grasped the crown of Pop's Beelzebub away from Sir Cliff and sat atop the throne as the official musical anti-Christ. For Jarvis Cocker and his band Pulp, to have come so far, and seen so many trends come and go, to be thwarted at the final hurdle by such a despicable beast was cruel justice.

Punk, New Romantics, C86, rave, baggy, shoe-gazing, new wave of new wave, and jungle had all been and gone while Pulp were soundchecking, and yet it was two crap actors who denied them at the gates of Pop Heaven. Pulp's greatest single, the era-defining 'Common People' had crashed in the charts at No 2, but was unable to usurp two actors from *Soldier Soldier* from the top spot. Still, for a band who had taken fourteen years to record what they called their début album, there was no rush.

Pulp always was and always will be Jarvis Cocker's band. Just as Blur are inextricably tied in with Damon Albarn's complex persona, Pulp will always revolve around Jarvis. As the band's only surviving original member, it is Jarvis who fronts the band, Jarvis who features in all the interviews, and Jarvis who is the focus on stage. Unavoidably, this is a severe injustice to the other members, but it is to Jarvis we must first turn.

One of the biggest attractions of Jarvis the sex god of 1995 is the sensuous doe-eyed smoulder he can seemingly hold forever. This is, in fact, the concentrated stare of a man with chronic myopia. Jarvis was not exactly a childhood heartthrob. He was born in the same year JFK was assassinated and twelve months before the British pop invasion of the United States, in Intake, a suburb of steel city Sheffield in 1963. Jarvis' parents were both artistic. His mother studied art, but despite some promise, she took up a 'proper job' emptying fruit machines as soon as Jarvis was born. His jovial trombone playing dad was less responsible. He was a small time musician and actor, who enjoyed most of his fame through a tenuous friendship with Sheffield's only rock hero, Joe Cocker, who despite the similarity in name was no relation of the family whatsoever. When Jarvis was seven his father left home and headed for Australia, where he secured a job as a DJ on the pretence he was Joe Cocker's brother. Life Down Under enabled him to avoid paying maintenance to Jarvis' mum. As part of a one parent family, the future Pulp singer was brought up in a predominantly female environment: his mother's friends used to congregate at his house for afternoon tea, and he found it difficult to relate to girls in the way that other boys did.

This wasn't helped by his geeky looks and his mother's frightening fashion sense. After a grave bout of meningitis had left his eyesight severely impaired at the age of five, he had to wear the thick-framed NHS spectacles which were the bane of every short-sighted Seventies school kid. This illness was probably the peak of his popularity, with all the school sending him Get Well cards and presents, all of which were later incincrated for fear of contamination. These thoughtful cards were rare – after this, he never once received a single Valentine card during his school years, a ritual humiliation for him.

To make matters worse, his loving mother dressed him in ridiculous leather shorts bought by a relative. With his long hair, bad teeth and angular bottle top glasses, Jarvis was an obvious target for school bullies. His lanky stature offered no physical protection, and in fact served to accentuate his oddness. He was the only boy at school who looked like an ugly girl. On top of all that his first name was a bully magnet, and his middle name, Branson, offered no respite. Still, it could have been worse – his younger sister was called Saskia, after Rembrandt's wife. Try explaining that to a Sheffield playground terrorist.

School days are notorious for fitting in or being left out. Childhood cruelty is very selective so by the time Jarvis was on the brink of his teens, he was a shy introverted loner. His mother worried about him, but he seemed happy enough in his bedroom, where he spent hours listening to the radio, taping songs and practising on a cheap guitar.

His interest in music led to him forming a band so, despite his school weirdo tag, he formed Arabicus Pulp (after a coffee bean commodity discussed during a dull Economics class) who didn't actually play, but existed to enable Jarvis to delegate roles to his mates. After a while, he and some friends bought a second-hand drum kit for £10 and rehearsed in his living room after school. 'Arabicus Pulp' was emblazoned across the bass drum shell. By 1979, with Jarvis now a towering fifth former, the band had something to show for all their efforts - not a gig but a Super 8 film including two surreal silent pieces called *The 300 Spartans* and *Spaghetti Western Meets Star Trek*. Bizarre or not, the film cost 10p to see and Arabicus Pulp made a handsome profit from their first public airing, earning Jarvis begrudging respect from his school tormentors.

Not that Jarvis was about to become Mr Popular. His forays into the outside world always reinforced his social alien status. When the clarion call for society's misfits arrived a couple of years before, in the shape of punk, Jarvis was captivated, and he tuned in to John Peel's show to keep up with the latest. His copy of The Stranglers' 'Rattus Norvegicus' was only dusted down to play when his mother was out. When he heard The Stranglers were playing the Sheffield Top Rank he had to go, but even here he was an outcast. "Believing in the punk spirit of individuality and self expression, I went along in a jumble sale jacket and a blue tie that my mother had crocheted for me," Jarvis later told *Melody Maker*. "All these people in mohicans just took the piss out of me and called me a mod." In a room full of identi-kit punks, Jarvis was once more the outsider.

The adolescent catalogue of disasters continued when his well-meaning mother got him his first job, scrubbing crabs at the fish market on Saturday mornings, not ideal at an age when hygiene and appearance are paramount. "It's not really the kind of job you want as a 16 year old who's desperate for a shag," Jarvis recounted later. "Even after you've gone home and had a bath you still smell of fish."

The only way he could cover up the smell was to douse himself in industrial detergent, hardly a teenage pheromone. His only taste of fitting in came when he went on holiday with the townies who also worked at the fish market – nobody minded the smell because they all reeked the same. On top of being too tall, with bad teeth, thick glasses and awful clothes, Jarvis stank as well. No wonder he never had a girlfriend at school.

Undeterred, an academically talented Jarvis stayed on at sixth form and achieved enough 'A' level grades to win a place to study English Literature at Liverpool University. This was certainly a chance to escape the drudgery of the seven hills of Sheffield and his small terraced house in run down Mansfield Road, but he turned it down. While his studies had been going well, so had his band. With an ever-shifting personnel, Arabicus Pulp had trimmed itself down to a suitably unfashionable monosyllabic Pulp, and started gigging locally. There had been an impromptu show during a chemistry lesson once, with a light show made up of burning lengths of magnesium ribbon, but the band's first genuine gig was at Rotherham Arts Centre in 1980. Stability was a perennial problem – original bassist David Lockwood had already left, and shortly after two more members left – a trait that hounded Jarvis until the mid-Eighties when he finally settled on the Pulp line-up of today. Local label Aardvark had refused Pulp's demo for a compilation album, but instead lined up this gig for them.In the meantime, Jarvis kept gigging the local toilet venues like the Hallamshire Hotel, The B-Hive, The Leadmill and The Limit, which had played host to The Police, U2 and even Simple Minds.

On the verge of undergraduate freedom, Jarvis probably declined his university place because he had been offered a prestigious John Peel session for Radio 1. Shortly before his 'A' level exams, Jarvis had been to see Peel DJ-ing at an unemployment benefit show at the Poly and had nervously handed him a tape of Pulp. The tape itself had been recorded by a local producer called Ken Patten who claimed he could reproduce the super-expensive vocoder vocal effect used at great expense by ELO through using an old war time microphone, a synth and 50p for a toilet roll.

It was a crude but worthy opening attempt, and Jarvis was not waiting by the phone for Peel's call. Being so used to rejection, he was amazed to return home one day to find his mom had been called by Peel's producer. Peel had listened to the Pulp demo in his car heading back down the M1 and was impressed enough to arrange a session for November 1981. The Pulp line-up of Jarvis, Peter Dalton, Jamie Pinchbecks and Wayne Furniss were guaranteed local celebrity when their decidedly odd music (played on borrowed gear) hit the airwaves, and the local indie label Armageddon expressed warm interest, but nothing evolved. Nevertheless, it was a glorious start. The band even got some press from this radio exposure, in *Melody Maker*. Jarvis told the magazine: "We just want to be on *Top Of The Pops* as soon as we can." It would be fourteen years before this ambition was realised.

This spasm of progress prompted Jarvis to defer and eventually abandon his academic career, and the Peel session in particular was used to convince his concerned mom that a long stint in further education would almost certainly snatch fame from his grasp. Unfortunately, it did not convince his fellow band members and all but Jarvis left for University, leaving him back at square one again. It was 1982.

Within a year and against the odds, Jarvis had written and recorded Pulp's début mini album, a naïve seven track affair called 'It'. The initial spurt of interest had eventually alerted the York-based Red Rhino Records, who offered to put out the album, much to Jarvis' delight. He scrabbled together a host of local musicians for the sessions, including Gary Wilson and Simon Hinkler of local band Artery (Hinkler went on to play guitar for arena-filling Goth lords The Mission - Hinkler co-wrote some of the material) and Tim Allcard (ex-In A Bell Jar). An oddball friend called Magnus took turns filling the drum stool. Jarvis' sister Saskia débuted on keyboards, as did Hinkler's younger brother David, making it more like a Jarvis collective. Even the recording sessions were fragmented, with one track being completed in the London studio owned by anarcho-punksters Crass.

Despite its unstable personnel, the band released 'It' in April 1983. It was an idealistic record, with a central theme of love and relationships which was ironic since Jarvis was yet to have a steady girlfriend. "I was just a kid when we made our first record, I hadn't even had sex," he admitted later. "I was writing about it, but I hadn't done anything."

The record received little press coverage and the little exposure it enjoyed was unsupportive – Jarvis' soporific lyrics came in for special criticism, most notably in *Melody Maker*, who justifiably stated: "The way Jarvis Cocker has expressed his thoughts in words makes the already lightweight music creak and collapse under the strain of slop and mush." Tracks like 'My Lighthouse' and 'Wishful Thinking' revealed a thinly-veiled obsession with love, a feature of all future Pulp records. On the positive side, it was a naïve but endearing release, in the same way that first love letters are naïve but endearing. To Jarvis now, it is an acute embarrassment.

Its shelf life was limited. The owner of Red Rhino later disappeared, as did the master tapes, and only 2000 copies were pressed. A single, the ill-fated 'Everybody's Problem', on which Jarvis bowed to then Pulp manager Tony Perrin's demand that he "sound like Wham", was awful and bombed completely.

Having opted out of University for Pulp, Jarvis expected some degree of success fairly soon. Unfortunately, for the next five years, he was the leader of a band on the dole, living in squalid conditions, changing members periodically, facing continued indifference from record companies and sharing his life with an increasingly weird array of local oddities and eccentrics. Fortunately, he was patient.

Mis-shapes, mistakes, misfits. Raised on a diet of baked beans. During this period of desolation, Jarvis lived in The Wicker, an old factory building that housed a cheap recording studio and some bedsits. At least Jarvis now had the core of the band, including Russell Senior. Russell had been desperate to join Pulp for some time and he hung around the band until he was finally accepted on guitar.

Around them in these grubby rooms were an alarming range of oddballs, drug users and general interlopers. One friend lived almost solely on baked beans. Another was obsessed with collecting enough spare parts to build a helicopter from scratch, whilst another dressed in a monk's outfit and kept a pet rat. Yet another ventured out in a Clockwork Orange-style boiler suit and was so badly beaten that he retreated into a weird life of military fixation and frighteningly disturbed paintings.

These weird surroundings did not deter Pulp from gigging sporadically throughout 1984 and 1985, including a show in a Leeds brothel and another gig, supposedly supported by a rugby-bloke's band called Ivor Biggun & The Hefty Cocks, although thankfully they didn't turn up. In the middle of this desperate period, Jarvis wrote and recorded a song at The Wicker that was something of a minor turning point in Pulp's career. It was called 'Little Girl (With Blue Eyes)' and it marked a considerable lyrical progression for the band. Chilling lines like "There's a hole in your heart and one between your legs, You've never had to wonder, which one he's going to fill" caused much furore in some quarters. Crucially, Candida Doyle joined on keyboards and provided an essential musical lift.

'Little Girl' won them a deal with London-based Fire Records, who agreed to release the track as a single, which they duly did in December of 1985. If the 'A' side wasn't controversial enough, the flip track 'The Will To Power' aroused suspicions of Nazi leanings. The unease deterred even John Peel from playing it, but sufficient publicity was garnered from the release to move Pulp one rung up the ladder. Interestingly enough, at a time when it was ultra-cool to be signed to an independent label, Jarvis made no bones about his ambitions, telling *Melody Maker*: "We want lots of people to buy our records. Being an indie band is like pottering around an allotment. We're not proud of our independence."

This ambition was based largely on Cocker's unswerving belief that he was destined to be a pop star and that the indie trenches were only a passing phase, a belief that manifested itself in his disinterest in everyday life and the mechanics of being 'normal', such as shopping. Unfortunately, this romanticism nearly killed him. One evening in 1985 he was at a party and was trying to impress a girl by hanging off a window ledge. Jim Morrison did it. Keith Moon did this stuff for breakfast. And then there's Iggy... Unfortunately Jarvis was none of these and fell three floors to the ground, smashing his pelvis, wrist, foot and suffering severe internal bruising as a result.

There followed a six week spell in a hospital ward full of old miners, where Jarvis was forced to lie back and reflect on his youthful dreams. While he was convalescing, a substantial change took place, as he later told *Vox* "That literally brought me down to earth. I had all the aestheticism beaten out of me. I thought I was sorted out to be a pop star. I had this very romanticised view of life, I'd never have to do anything practical. Then I fell out of this window."

Once out of hospital, Jarvis faced two months in a wheelchair as his shattered foot repaired. He had been told he would never walk properly again but in the event he recovered fully. In the meantime, no Pulp gigs were cancelled – instead Jarvis performed in a wheelchair, twitching to the music with frenetic hand movements. At a time when Morrissey was provoking outrage for making a hearing aid a fashion accessory, this was a heavyweight celebrity disability which some saw as a sick parody of The Smiths frontman. It wasn't, but at least this spell on wheels taught Jarvis how to command an audience with just his hands.

It was a classic absurdist turning point. While in hospital Jarvis voraciously read Tom Wolfe, whose attention to detail and ability to make the most mundane subjects burst with energy and excitement fascinated him. "He made stuff I might have dismissed as crap seem exciting – stories about stock car racing or surfers," Jarvis later told interviewers. "It was a revelation. Reality wasn't this grey lump of concrete after all. It's been my personal thing ever since to try and do that." From hereon, Pulp records were never the same again.

The time was not yet right for Pulp to orbit, however. Much to Jarvis' annoyance, The Smiths and New Order had been holding court with observational brilliance that shattered anything Pulp had up their sleeve. Even so, the next Pulp album, 'Freaks', which didn't come out until May 1987, was another notch up the ladder. It was an appropriate title for a disturbing album. Some clues to the darker direction could be gleaned from the preceding single 'Dogs Are Everywhere', released in June 1986, which was a disturbed, paranoid observation about the animal in everyone. Jarvis said at the time: "I'll tell you one thing about Pulp, we're not about being grey and dull, but we do a lot of wallowing in the dirt, we want to convey the love in the egg, chips and beans, we want to carve something between the lines of the everyday world." It was a pensive, odd track and, when followed by the equally perverse singles 'Masters Of The Universe' (a worrying Nietzschean control freak-out) and 'They Suffocate At Night' (lambasting the claustrophobia of close relationships), suggested that Jarvis was already on his way down the path of scary pop subversive.

This warning was delivered in full when 'Freaks' was released. It was a dark, humourless record, full of mordant, twisted music. The central theme was summarised in the sub-title of 'Ten Songs about Power, Claustrophobia, Suffocation and Holding Hands'. There was a pasteboard of freaks, misfits and discontent here. 'The Never Ending Story' documented a failed love affair, 'I Want You' saw love as a catastrophic immolation, and 'Anorexic Beauty' was chillingly weird. It was a peculiarly parochial collection of morose oddballs amongst the parking meters, seedy flats and mundane council estates.

The backdrop to this record was that Jarvis was very unhappy. He felt the album had decent songs but was poorly recorded and unrepresentative. The band atmosphere was sour, and a few months later there were yet more personnel changes. He was still living in the rat-infested Wicker and felt himself to be one of the freaks of the album's title. The recording itself was miserable, for with only £600 to spend, all they could afford was a cheap 8-track studio with only one microphone. The end result was a poor imitation of the band's increasingly powerful live show. Jarvis had left school years ago, but now he was beginning to doubt himself for the first time. He later told the media: "I definitely felt I had taken the wrong turn at that point, and that album was all about that feeling. I was living in this weird place and all the strange characters of Sheffield used to come round, it just seemed that we were all becoming freaks that weren't legitimate members of society and I hated that. I didn't want it to happen." He also said: "I didn't go to University to do the band, and for five years nothing had happened. I was having to face the terrible possibility that I'd made a mistake." One gig in Derby while they were recording the album was attended by only two people. Perhaps it *had* all been a mistake.

Most annoying of all was the apparent disservice the album did to the Pulp live show. Over the years, the band's interest in the performing arts had brought a surreal quality to their gigs, which was now complemented by genuinely disturbing music. The Pulp collection of stage turns is a weird and wonderful one. At various points in their career they have wrapped the entire stage gear in toilet paper/crepe paper and/or silver foil, kicked silver footballs into the crowd, handed out doughnuts and fruit, delivered obscure monologues about flying into space, recited surreal poetry, spun fishing lines around the band, dangled apple cores from their guitars, and played a ten minute introduction of white noise. One stage set saw them play behind giant picture frames made from footwear, probably the nearest Pulp ever came to shoe-gazing. Another time they performed one of Russell's plays, which culminated in Jarvis eating a plate of dog shit at an interview. Perhaps most odd was the phase when, instead of introducing each song, Jarvis would hang another item on a washing line that was strung across the stage, which frequently became laden down with fruit, plastic limbs and space-age stars. The accompanying musical live performance was odd in itself – violins clashing with stylophones and ringing guitars, all mixed together with a thrashing drummer and a trembling crooner of a singer who looked like a Zimmer frame inside a second hand suit.

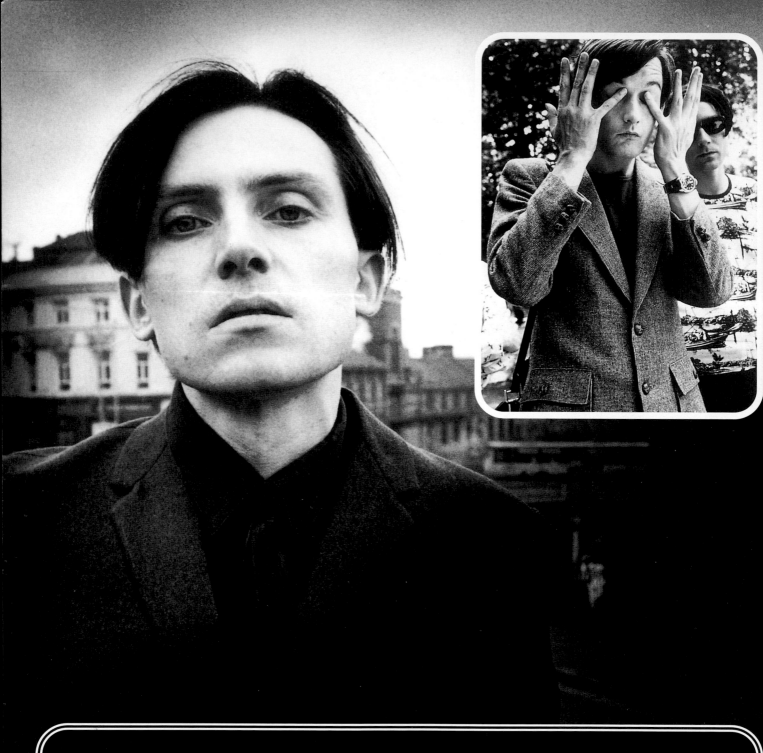

In such a suffocating environment, there was really only one thing that Jarvis could do – move out of Sheffield. So in 1988 he enrolled at St. Martin's in London on a film course, despite the fact that Candida and Nick Banks remained in Sheffield. If six weeks hospitalisation had been one turning point, this bold move was perhaps the most important of all, as Jarvis himself told journalists later: "The move to London was when Pulp really began in earnest, because that was when I finally realised I didn't want to be like those characters (in Sheffield). I wanted to be more popular and attractive." On one level the move cemented the principal Pulp line-up with fellow College student Steve Mackay becoming a permanent bassist. The band now had a concrete shape. On another level, Jarvis' experiences at St. Martin's provided the artistic catalyst to propel Pulp on to success, as he explained to the music papers later: "It was great, it really focused me on what I was. Suddenly you had to think about everything again, and that's what made the band really, it gave us material."

During his time at St. Martin's, Jarvis made several films including one about an angel who came to earth and ended up in a pub singing competition; he and Steve also set up a film company which produced videos for, amongst others, Aphex Twin. He also donned contact lenses, which must have been an almighty liberating experience.

Conversely, he found the anonymity of the Big Smoke intimidating, and didn't have sex for the first three years after moving there. Another experience was Jarvis' temporary absorption in the blossoming rave scene during 1988's summer of love. He was bowled over by the 'one love' sentiment at these parties and indulged in ecstasy occasionally. Not having been one for scenes, Jarvis was unusually involved: "I surprised myself by how much I got into it. I'd never been particularly into trends before. No way was I being a goth. And I couldn't be a new romantic – I would have looked a tit in knickerbockers." One particularly funny night spent raving saw Jarvis take a bad E and he spent all the evening singing Milli Vanilli songs then woke up thinking he was Paul Nicholas.

Moving to London had effectively put Pulp on hold, and the band went into semi-hibernation. With two of the band in London, and the other three in Sheffield, rehearsals were virtually impossible, gigs were even rarer and progress slowed to a virtual stop. Nick Banks, now permanently in the drum seat, was in full-time teaching, Candida Doyle was working in a toy shop, and Russell Senior, after a brief and ill-fated spell in London, moved back up north to work in antique glass. After nearly ten years of relentless slog, Pulp just stopped trying so bloody hard. And the world started to take notice.

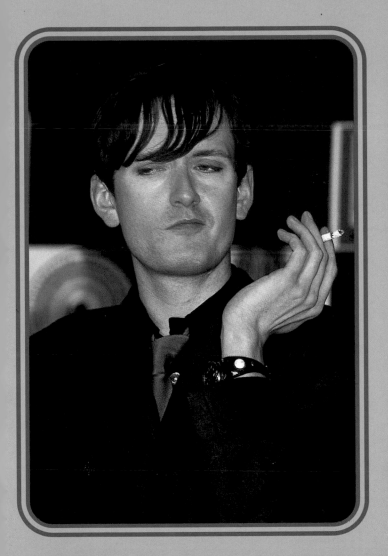

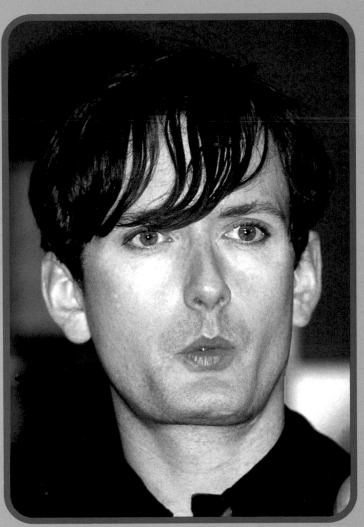

A year after starting College, Jarvis and Pulp re-signed to Fire Records after a brief period away, and began a spell of rapid progress. Two class singles, supported by a run of stunning live shows, and a subsequent trio of singles on a new label meant that by the end of Jarvis' college course the pop world was in awe, and the major labels were flocking to Pulp's door.

The first of the two singles was perhaps Pulp's finest moment thus far: 'My Legendary Girlfriend', a simple, captivating tune concealing yet another disturbing tale of sublime oddity. It was a throbbing lament, as much influenced by Barry White, Van McCoy and fellow Sheffield popsters The Human League as anything else, an absurdly unfashionable lineage at this time of fraggle rock domination. Augmented by rude noises from Jarvis, it was mysterious and pompous, yet clear and simple. For Pulp's so-called comeback single after Jarvis' relocation to the capital and subsequent quiet spell, it was a mini classic and *NME* acknowledged it as such by making it their Single of the Week.

The next single, 'Countdown', added to the array of Pulp material that was now gathering pace. Written while Jarvis was in hospital, it described the countdown to life's single defining moment and the morbid recognition that quite often nothing better ever follows. It was an amazing, terrifyingly drunken disco anthem, painful but brilliant. With releases like these, Pulp gigs were gradually becoming places worth going to.

The live show was the perfect parallel to the superb material Pulp were producing. Their gigs around the end of the Eighties and early Nineties were the subject of critical acclaim rarely matched by their peers. Review after review praised their unique sound, their bizarre and still highly unfashionable appearance, the band's tremendous ability, the humorous and subversive lyrics and of course, Jarvis' rapidly developing stage craft. *Melody Maker* raved: "The real stars of the evening are glamsters Pulp, exquisite intricate melodramas, excruciating and outrageously (un)sexy. This man has more star potential in his signet ring than Damon of Blur will have in a lifetime." Jarvis himself was quite clear what his goals for the live performance were, as he explained to *NME*: "You listen to Radio 2, well I do anyway, and they play Matt Munro, Engelbert Humperdinck and stuff that doesn't really get made anymore. It's a bit clichéd so that is why people think it is cheesy – but the reason why people performed in that way is because it is quite effective, if you can break through the cheese barrier, you can make contact."

The third stage in this renaissance came after Jarvis left College and the band signed to Sheffield's Gift Records (a spin off from Aphex Twin's home of Warp Records) for three singles, which catapulted Pulp into a major record deal and on to the brink of substantial success in the space of a year. Originally intended to raise the band's profile on the continent, the trio of classics started with 'OU' which revealed more of the strange upside down universe of Jarvis Cocker. The doubt and pain were still there, but the avalanche of organs and fizzing stylophone, and the ascending chord climax made the track a colossal, immensely attractive number. This was not kitsch, this was real life. More Single of the Week accolades followed, although the song was slightly overshadowed by Suede's infamous début as the best new band in Britain with 'The Drowners' – how Jarvis must have wondered what he had to do when he saw a band barely a year old sharing his limelight.

Both bands shared a degree of disdain for their surroundings but Suede's London-centric viewpoint was a more fashionable parochialism, and Brett Anderson's ambiguous sexuality and retro performance was hailed as infinitely more appealing than the synthetic atrocities, glitter balls and Farfisa organs offered by Jarvis the Geek. Heroic failure snapped at the heels of success again for Pulp, who appeared destined to languish in the commercial no man's land of cult credibility.

But Pulp would just not give up. 'OU' was followed by an even better track, the modern cracker 'Babies'. Some said it was Pulp's finest moment and they may have been right. With Jarvis' lubricious baritones, lyrical nostalgia, the minutiae of suburban life, sordid sex, peculiar synths and lurching bass and guitar, this had all the archetypal elements of a Pulp track, yet it was far from self-parody. The tale of a boyfriend watching his girlfriend's sister shagging from a wardrobe and then being forced to have sex with her was perhaps the sort of dramatic, well-sculpted narrative that no other band except Pulp would have attempted. Its musical awkwardness belied a serious, seedy undertone of genuine erotic charge, a sexually cool restraint that was far mightier than Anderson's fey headline grabbing. With B-side 'Sheffield – Sex City' listing in breathy whispers a litany of northern towns during one man's day and night on heat, Jarvis' lyrical advances were accelerating. Sardonic words were easily interpreted but far from being shallow, they were monumental.

If 'Babies' hadn't won you over, then 'Razzmatazz' certainly would. Coming in early 1993, this single continued Jarvis' lyrical deftness and the theme a synthetic suburbia full of tawdry affairs and the absurd modern tragedies of real life. This was perhaps the most scary of the three releases – a pop record on the surface but underneath there were clear sightings of incest, family intimidation and pre-pubescent deviance. The flip side trilogy called 'Inside Susan' was perhaps even more impressive than the lead track. With yet another Single of the Week accolade, Pulp had successfully chipped away at public indifference and attracted the sort of attention their music had been striving for for years.

The rave live reviews continued to flood in, and were complemented by the cultivation of a 'mad' Jarvis image. This was the bonkers Suede that was waiting to be discovered. His between-song patter, ugly suits and emaciated chest, coupled with the weird stage sets, made Pulp far more entertaining to watch than their peers. On the down side, there were certain complications that slowed down progress. Firstly, they were locked in an angry legal battle with Fire Records that sapped their energy and resources and would not be settled for some time. Distribution problems had already affected the release of *Freaks* and the single 'My Legendary Girlfriend' but there had been an unbelievable delay for their *Separations* album, which they had made way back in 1989 but which Fire had not released until 1992. This was right in the middle of Pulp's new phase when they felt the material on that postponed album was already sorely anachronistic. The twisted neurosis of songs like 'My Legendary Girlfriend' and 'Countdown' was impressive enough, but the album was filled with embryonic sketchy tracks which the band now saw as having little relation to the new Pulp.

Secondly, Pulp were uncomfortably tagged on to the end of a Seventies revival scene that included bands like Suede, Denim and St. Etienne, and which somebody for some unknown reason tried to call either Lion Pop (sounds like an ice cream) or, more logically, The Crimplene Scene. Jarvis didn't help matters by saying things like "The Seventies were very tacky, people would be wearing vinyl jackets and getting a bit sweaty, at least the Seventies were sexy, whereas in the Eighties everyone just watched *The Antiques Roadshow*." But the tenuous link between these bands was never going to fully accommodate Pulp. Some tried semantics, with one writer calling them "an eccentric techno space pop miserabilist northern electro cabaret troupe", others simply called them kitsch, but both were wrong. The third blow to their upwardly mobile status was having all their gear stolen from a van in Peckham.

Nevertheless Pulp's live reputation continued to grow, swelling the ever-expanding fan base that was being won over by the volley of superb singles. Dave Stewart and his ex-Bananarama wife Siobhan were sighted at one gig, the band's Sheffield Sound City gig was a stormer, and then Pulp astounded thousands at the Finsbury Park festival headlined by The Cult. Most impressive was their performance during their March 1993 support slot to current faves St. Etienne, which coincided with the release of 'Razzmatazz'. Quite simply, Pulp blew the thin sounding headliners off stage night after night. It was high theatre but not, as some said, cheap comedy. Despite Jarvis' acidic humour, Pulp took themselves very seriously indeed. Beneath the one-liners and quips lay a set of songs that barely hid a wounded, deflated heart and an observational mind not seen since Morrissey's heyday. By mid-1993, Pulp's resurrection as purveyors of pop eccentricity was nearly complete. The usually subdued Jarvis even acknowledged the progression that was made during this crucial twelve month period when he told to the music media: "That was the beginning of a new era, we got invited to play loads of concerts and the scene was totally different. And people actually liked us."

The summer of 1993 was a quiet period for Pulp, but this time with good reason. The continued acclaim had finally brought offers of a major label deal and Island, home to the world's biggest band U2, finally won the band's signatures. Ironically, after their troubles with Fire, the first release on this new label was a re-issue! Fortunately, this time it was with the band's backing, as Island gathered together the three Gift EP's, with B-sides, and put out the album 'Pulp – Intro' which came as a mid-price package at £7.00. This served a twofold purpose, scuppering the rising prices on the Gift series imports, and introducing the band to the public through the mass marketing muscle of a major. As a composite record, the three Gift releases were disturbingly sexy and merely confirmed what many people had now begun to suspect: that Pulp were on the verge of becoming Britain's best band.

Jarvis was typically more realistic – after over a decade of not selling records, and six years since the band's last album, he was not about to get carried away, as he told the impressed music weeklies. "Now we totally fail or succeed. With indie labels it's okay if you don't sell many records because you're artistically valid and doing what you want, and you can stay in your own ghetto. It can't be like that with a major – we signed to them, they gave us money, we must sell records." Nick Banks was a little more upbeat, saying. "The thing to remember is that we've been going so long now we've established our own internal sub-culture we can depend on."

During the tail end of 1993 and all of 1994, the success of Pulp's early singles and album for the major label caused the band's popularity to rocket to such an extent that by the year's end they were handed platinum album discs and a Mercury Award nomination. The escalation started with their first single, 'Lipgloss' which surfaced in November 1993. It was another tale of grim reality, beautifully detailed unrequited love portraying everyday lives ebbing wastefully away, mixed with a celebration of the strangeness of the mundane. The keyboard loopiness and slashing guitars mixed with the quirky drum beat made this another compelling and highly idiosyncratic, unerringly poppy Pulp release. The ten minute epic 'Deep Fried In Kelvin' flip side was a typically bizarre addition. A few dissenting voices called it cartoon Pulp, but for the vast majority it was a delicious major label début and it was followed by a sold-out 14 date UK tour and an appearance on the late night show *The Word*. Unfortunately, chart success narrowly eluded them, but Pulp didn't care – they knew what was coming next.

Do you remember the first time? Jarvis does, he had to wait twenty years for it. So when Pulp released their next single with this highly personal question as the title, they decided to put some people on the spot. So alongside the normal video for the single, the band recorded a 26-minute film of portrait interviews with a variety of celebrities. Among the list of stars revealing all about their virginal breakthrough were John Peel, Jo Brand, Vic Reeves and Bob Mortimer, Justine from Elastica and Terry Hall, as well as Candida's mom, who was just passing! The fascinating revelations were premiered in March 1994 at the prestigious ICA in London (where the band played a brief six song set) and generated much publicity for Pulp, particularly with snippets such as Jo Brand describing banging her head on the toilet and Terry Hall nearly being put off because his partner was a Bay City Roller fan.

As promo's go it was brilliant, reflecting Steve and Jarvis' film-based college backgrounds. Many bands would have struggled to match this visual paean to your first shag with the corresponding single, but Pulp did so with consummate ease. 'Do You Remember The First Time?' was not only Pulp's best single to date, it was their début Top 40 hit as well. The frilly guitars and shaky, urgent vocals detailed the darkly amusing theme of a song that was wrapped in sleek pop glitter. Pulp had finally arrived, after a fourteen year wait.

Having broken their chart duck, Pulp became a permanent feature. Recording started on what the band themselves classed as their 'debut' album in August 1993, and although the original release date was Valentine's Day 1994, the record finally emerged in April, the week after Kurt Cobain committed suicide. Entitled 'His 'n' Hers', this album marked Pulp's ascent to the very forefront of British pop, with a breathtaking collection of singles and album tracks. Once again, the backdrop to the record was behind-the-net-curtains working class Britain, littered with odd sexual mores, libidinous deviancy and suburban nastiness, musically and lyrically documented in finer detail than on any previous Pulp record.

There was the grandeur of the singles 'Do You Remember', 'Babies' and 'Lipgloss' obviously, but they were not the stand-out tracks. 'Acrylic Afternoons' was a celebratory salute to housing estate afternoon sex, 'Pink Glove' suggested dressing up to rejuvenate a tired sex life, and 'Have You Seen Her Lately?' was full of the precise details of ultra-normality that Tom Wolfe had so inspired in a convalescing Jarvis. The libidinous protagonist of 'She's A Lady' two-timed his young girlfriend with an older woman, and elsewhere there were tales of deceit and sordid affairs. Musically there was great variety, from the croonerish ballroom ballad 'Happy Ending' to the the speeding disco Hi-NRG of 'She's A Lady'. Jarvis' breathy inflections and spoken vocals worked finer than ever before, and the sonic background was full of disco gurgles, car boot stylophones, kazoos, woozy violins, odd keyboard arrangements and even a fire extinguisher!

Lyrically the first person tales contrasted sharply to the May 1994 album of the year 'Parklife', whose writer Damon Albarn shared a similar fascination with the perversity of modern life, albeit through a third person narrative. The overall effect was a very funny, very tragic observation of British, parochial (sex) lives, and although Jarvis visited his now familiar themes of futile love, illicit lust and man-made fibres, there was a new desperation, a keener degree of distress about these characters, and an undertone of casual violence. For a band so old, this sounded remarkably fresh. For a supposed joke band, this was frightening stuff. Crafted in a twisted niche that was all their own, this was Pulp's darkest, grittiest, most realistic album yet. It was also their finest.

Commercially the album hit No.9 in the charts, a triumph for Britain's worst kept musical secret. The critical acclaim that greeted the album was accompanied by huge sales – by the end of the year 'His 'n' Hers' had achieved platinum status. At last it seemed that Pulp were joining the highest echelons of pop. After ten years as bridesmaids, it was their turn to take the limelight. Even with Blur's landmark 'Parklife' taking most of the honours, 'His 'n' Hers' was a regular feature in the 1994 Polls (and Jarvis was even creeping up the 'Sexiest Man' listings) and was nominated for the prestigious Mercury Music Award. Incredibly, this award for so-called new music went to M People, but Pulp lost by only one vote. Jarvis was suitably deadpan in his after dinner comments when he told *NME*: "If we'd won, we'd have split the money five ways and it would have gone to charity in the end because I buy all my clothes from Oxfam and Barnado's." He wasn't joking – when the band were given a clothing budget on signing to Island, Jarvis couldn't see anything he fancied in the department stores and ending up buying two 50p jackets from the local Cancer Research shop.

On a more serious note, 'His 'n' Hers' ushered in a period of tremendous growth for Pulp. They played at Sound City in Glasgow, a performance that was broadcast live on Radio 1; they played Glastonbury for the first time, producing a stormer of a set; their 11 date album tour sold out in hours; they were the highlight of the Reading festival weekend and they supported Blur at their triumphant Alexandra Palace show in October, perhaps the only band capable of doing so in 1994. And they released 'The Sisters' EP, another bitter and twisted collection of debonair fantasies.

In addition, Jarvis became something of a media personality throughout the year. He appeared on *Pop Quiz* alongside Des'ree and Chesney Hawkes (the one and only) and won with sheer (pissed) brilliance. *Top Of The Pops* producers were impressed by Jarvis' word-for-word recital of a John Miles piece and invited him to present their show, which he did complete with an "I hate Wet Wet Wet" sign inside his suitably unfashionable jacket. Marti Pellow dismissed Pulp as indie nobodies, but no-one else seemed to agree. Pulp played some excellent low key charity shows for the London Lighthouse Aids charity along with Neneh Cherry and Holly Johnson. They appeared at the *Pulp Fiction* premiere and met Tarantino himself, and they rounded off an amazing year by playing a special Christmas show at the Drury Lane theatre normally reserved for *Miss Saigon*. Hardly the sort of year indie nobodies have. Oh, and Jarvis moved out of his council house in Camberwell to a flat in Ladbroke Grove, so fame definitely went to his head. He even bumped into the magician David Copperfield waiting for the lift in a London hotel lobby but resisted the enormous temptation to ask him why he didn't simply fly up to his floor.

For the others, it was also welcome relief, as Russell told interviewers: "For the entirety of the Eighties we had to have a whip around to spend 15 hours in the back of a cold transit van to play to 12 people. Don't let anyone romanticise about it, its a load of rubbish, best off out of it." Nick was even more direct about his old lifestyle: "You'd get up in the morning feeling like you'd been shat out of a horse."

The other members of Pulp always take a back seat to their enigmatic frontman, but musically they are crucial to the band' success. Russell (two years Jarvis') Senior, who has been with Jarvis the longest, graduated from Bath University with Business Studies in 1982, the year before he joined the band. He still lives in Sheffield with his girlfriend and two children. Since 1983 he has provided much needed guitar textures and melodic inspiration to Jarvis' basic lyrics – the band usually produce the music first. His violin playing, although less frequent nowadays, was a key feature of early Pulp.

Candida Doyle, the lone female who has to tolerate laddish behaviour on tour, is the same age as Jarvis, and joined briefly after Russell. She has become increasingly accomplished at dealing with the music press and the machinations of being a star, and is now perhaps Pulp's most ambitious member. Her keyboard playing is crucial to the Pulp sound, and her odd choice of gear, Farfisas and old Moog synths, is central to their success.

Nick Banks finally gave up his wreath making to concentrate on Pulp full-time, and apparently has a bass drum full of ladies underwear that has been thrown on stage. He endured much peer pressure as a younger musician to earn an honest living, but now that Pulp's success has taken them on to the nation's television screens, his life is considerably more comfortable.

Steve Mackey joined Pulp after meeting Jarvis at St. Martin's. His fluid bass playing suits Pulp's stylistically and his shocking resemblance to Alex James from Blur is sometimes the only question he gets asked. The newest member is Mark Webber, a long time fan of the band who originally wrote and ran their fanzine. He became their tour manager and grew to be such an integral part of the set-up that they finally offered him the chance to join on second guitar for live performances in 1992.

If Pulp were pleased with the events of 1994, it was nothing compared to what awaited them in 1995. The signs had all been there – the gigs in the spring were unusually vibrant, and the band appeared to have a new self-confidence. Although their attire was somewhat more sober, their performance of the forthcoming material was as flamboyant as ever.

Nothing could have prepared them for the reaction to their first single from the new sessions, 'Common People' in June 1995. Released as a double A-side with the superb 'Underwear', all eyes were on 'Common People' with its true life tale of a rich Greek girl wanting to slum it with Jarvis at art college. Apparently the only fiction was that the real girl never wanted to sleep with him! It was one of Britpop's defining moments – 1995's 'Girls & Boys' – and rocketed Pulp on to the main playlists of every major radio station in the country. The reaction when it was first aired at Reading in 1994 had been excellent, but this was incredible. Suddenly Pulp found themselves the most

in-demand group, especially with Oasis and Blur both in-between albums. Jarvis expressed high hopes for this single in interviews for the release: "We knew that was a special song as soon as we started playing it live. People would always come up to us after gigs and talk about it. You don't write a song like that everyday." Oddly enough, Island hadn't wanted to release it because they felt it was too far in advance of the autumn scheduled album. Commercially it was huge, with only Robson & Jerome preventing Pulp's first No.1 single, and the expectations it built for the new album were massive. Even after the considerable success of 'His 'n' Hers', Pulp were still unacceptable to many sectors but with the enormous success of 'Common People' they were suddenly household names. "It's nice to know people are actually listening and waiting for the new album," said Jarvis. "A few years ago we were just releasing things into a vacuum." The song itself was a Europop narrative mixed with an anthemic chorus to beat all-comers, and it clearly defined the envy/snobbery dynamic of so many people. Many thought it was 1995's finest single.

Pulp had planned to leave the summer almost free of festivals or gigs, so that work on the new album could progress without distraction, but this was not to be. After The Stone Roses appalling last-minute withdrawal from a headline slot at Glastonbury, Pulp were asked to fill the spot that several others, including Rod Stewart and Blur, had turned down. Pulp were more than happy to oblige. "I don't mind that they asked other people to fill the slot before us," Jarvis told *NME*. "I'm just glad it's us. The thing that's important is that we get to go there and be a part of it. You'll find us in Yellow Pages under Bands For Hire. We're the super-subs of modern music."

Pulp were not just a part of the 25th Glastonbury – more than any other band, they represented the entire weekend's celebrations. After an ignominious start, where they had to hire a cheap van because all the pop star types had rented the expensive ones, Pulp took a wrong turn and landed smack bang in the middle of a field full of people trying to watch Sleeper. The band had declined a top hotel and opted to hire tents for the weekend, and although rumours of a gold lame tent for the Jarv were rife, he made do with a normal plastic roof. They were pestered all weekend by fans and because they refused to have security guards, at times this was quite worrying. Three hours before the performance, Jarvis could be found sitting in his tent alone, putting his contact lenses in and trying to relax. Robbie Williams and Damien Hirst dropped in to wish him luck but he remained edgy. He later said this was the most nervous he had ever been.

He needn't have worried – Pulp's set was rapturously received and the climax of 'Common People', with 100,000 singing along nearly reduced Jarvis to tears. In hippy central a gangly man dressed in a suit and tie had commanded the huge crowd like no-one else that weekend. If this was why Pulp had slogged all those years and fought to be heard, then it was finally and unreservedly worthwhile. Before the rendition of 'Common People' Jarvis said "If a lanky git like me can headline Glastonbury, then anyone can." At the end of the set, Jarvis walked to the front of the stage and said: "This just proves that if you believe in something strongly enough it will happen." After the gig, Jarvis told waiting reporters: "I have never experienced anything like that before, everyone was singing really loud, that was a lot of people who knew all the words. That's when success seemed real. Undeniable. Concrete evidence. It did move me."

With typical pragmatism, Pulp were in the studio recording the new album early Monday morning after the Glastonbury weekend. Over the next few months however, there were more distractions as the band's popularity and notoriety rocketed. The popularity explosion that 'Common People' started saw Pulp all over magazine covers and television screens nearly all year. With Jarvis now firmly established as something of a fashion and sex icon, Pulp appeared at the *Smash Hits* awards to ear-piercing screams, yet still effortlessly commanded the audience at the alternative Heineken Festival (christened Britstock) alongside indie peers such as Skunk Anansie and Menswear. Although the band did not contribute to the War Child album 'Help', Jarvis did design some hand-made shoes for the corresponding Pagan Fun Wear fashion show. They fetched the highest price of the night at £5100, more than bikinis by Dave Stewart and trousers by David Bowie. *The Big Breakfast* staged a National Jarvis Day, and on the back of his catwalk debut, Jarvis was asked to model for Katherine Hamnett in Milan, something he would have loved to do but was too busy. He co-presented the cutting edge Radio 1 *Evening Session* with Steve Lamacq and graced the front covers of teen mags, pop weeklies and style bibles like *The Face*. Pulp, the perennial misfits, were now one of Britain's biggest bands, and Jarvis Cocker the awkward, geeky school weirdo was one of the nation's grooviest sex gods. Justice at last.

In the peculiar manner of the 'build them up and then knock them down' mentality, once Pulp had arrived at the pinnacle of pop, the tabloids sought to demolish what they had worked so hard to achieve. Their first target was the second single of the new campaign, the double A-side 'Sorted For E's & Wizz/Mis-Shapes'. Those who bothered to read the lyrics and listen to the track knew it was no pro-drugs song, but the tabloids superficially misread its intentions and whipped up a public frenzy about this supposedly callous drug peddling band called Pulp. The scene of the crime, so to speak, was the record sleeve, which they alleged showed how to make a drugs wrap. Jarvis patiently explained it was considerably less harmful. "Basically it's an origami diagram," Jarvis told *NME*. "I may be wrong, but as far as I know, there are no recorded instances of origami leading to drug addiction." More seriously, he added: "The single was originally going to be in a wrap, but that proved too costly, so we thought we'd stick to origami. I don't agree with putting severed babies heads on record sleeves, that's too easy. This just seemed appropriate because it's a record about drugs."

The tabloids missed this point altogether... it was about drugs, neither pro- nor anti. The *Daily Mirror* was horrified and slapped Jarvis' face on the front page with the banner headline "Ban This Sick Stunt". Jarvis issued a statement explaining himself, but it was too late. The offending record sleeve was withdrawn and a plain sleeve used instead. Jarvis was amazed at the over-reaction and accusations of promoting drug dealing, and simply said "Drugs? I'd rather peddle my bicycle." Ironically the title was taken from a conversation with a girl who had seen The Stone Roses at Spike Island and said that phrase was a constant feature of the night.

The song was a backwards glance at the late Eighties rave scene that had initially captivated Jarvis and later revealed itself as something of a sham. As far as the tabloids were concerned, Jarvis was virtually a fully paid up member of the Cali Cartel and nothing short of full castration would suffice. Fortunately this wasn't a view shared by the majority, including Radio 1, who refused to ban it. Consequently the single hit the No. 2 spot just like its predecessor, with advance sales of 200,000 (Island's highest ever, including U2). All the *Daily Mirror* had succeeded in doing was to create an instant collector's record sleeve.

Now all eyes were on Pulp, which was perfect because next up was their new album. They probably couldn't have generated such expectations if they had wanted (or had they?). With the already-legendary Glastonbury performance fuelling hopes for the new record, and the two superb singles preceding it, the next Pulp album had to be good. It wasn't good, it was brilliant.

'Different Class' was as apt a title as any, both in terms of their peers and relative to their own previous material. Its scope was much broader than the provincial 'His 'n' Hers' and although many of the key themes remained the same, the delivery and musicality of the record far surpassed anything that Pulp had produced before. Alongside the sex, there was now revenge and class. Songs like 'Common People' and 'Mis-Shapes' were alongside such stunning pieces as 'I Spy', a track on which the jilted Jarvis savagely pays back for every jibe and every slight he has experienced by shagging his enemy's wife, smoking his fags, sleeping in his bed and even enjoying the contemplation of being caught. Written while Jarvis was on the dole, this sustained drama was truly hateful. This was Pulp's darkest track yet, intensely perverse and disturbing.

There was more seediness on 'Underwear' in which the central character is about to be caught *en flagrente*, and brooding ballads like 'Live Bed Show' and 'Pencil Skirt'. Jarvis was the loser in love yet again on the stunning 'Disco 2000' but perhaps most notably there was finally a Pulp track of genuine mutual love, with 'Feelings Called Love' offering the first glimmer of hope for the constant loner that had stalked Pulp's previous work. The flights of fancy sat right next to clinically accurate observations on real life, and the wry humour was only just visible amongst this collection of more universal yet genuinely subversive and dramatic takes on life.

Musically the album ranged enormously. The clutch of pop classics compared with any contemporary record, and with the flamboyant and lyrically exemplary 'Disco 2000', Pulp had produced a single to rival the mighty 'Common People' if that were possible. There were the obscure discordant tracks such as 'I Spy' as well as the more traditional structures, but even here the climactic verses and monumental choruses added an extra element. There was even the uniquely elegiac 'Bar Italia' – it was all here. The album maintained an implausibly high plateau throughout, and elevated Pulp's often sinister pop vision to new and greater heights. The caustic lyrics and biting titles signalled Jarvis' true graduation as a passionate songsmith of genuine high calibre. He had had the lyrics floating in his head for many months, but they all came together in a two day brainstorming session drinking cheap brandy and chain smoking at his sister's flat. This wasn't cheap platitudes and patronising truisms however, but sincere wisdom gained through years of living this very life. With 'Different Class', Pulp had made a landmark album.

The elaborately packaged album, with 12 different covers included in each record, went straight in the charts at No. 1 and went platinum within its first week of sales. It captured the elusive 'zeitgeist' perfectly, giving Britpop's most militant misfits a colossal commercial smash. All this was ten years to the week since Jarvis fell out of a window and was hospitalised trying to impress someone. No need for that anymore.

The band were clearly very proud of the record, rightly so. Jarvis was adamant that his formative years of struggling were the key when told interviewers: "I didn't leave Sheffield until I was 25, by which time I was a fully formed sad adult, so I'd been formed by Sheffield. That's what 'Different Class' is all about." In another interview he emphasised the contrast between life in Sheffield and London. "It's less obsessed with sad relationships, it's about situations I've been in since coming to London, from living in a squat in Mile End to going to a party at Gianni Versace's." Either way, he was not about to listen to any more claims that Pulp were ironic or a joke band. "I haven't devoted 15 years of my life to a joke. You may think we are totally misguided but we are totally honest. Anyone who has listened properly should realise that we were *never* tongue in cheek."

With the huge success of 'Different Class' propelling Pulp into the Super League of British pop, the album tour (their first in over a year) and subsequent arena tour in the new year of 1996 were sold out in a matter of a few hours. There were yet more television appearances for Jarvis and the band, another Peel interview (this time at the DJ's home) and a prestigious session on *Later With Jools Holland*, complete with 16 piece orchestra. European dates and TV slots followed, as did an almost stalker-like mentality from the tabloids, who were now reduced to trying to set Jarvis up by allegedly paying kids to offer him drugs with a camera man in the bushes ready and waiting. There was an odd incident where local police in Brighton removed the album cover and surrounding artwork from a gay book shop window, saying the name Cocker in that context was offensive! There was also a minor incident in Bridlington where police were somewhat heavy handed with fans, having taken the tabloid dictum of Jarvis the Jackal rather too literally. Otherwise, this was another incredibly successful period for Pulp, fuelled by the release of the new single of the grooviest Pulp track ever, 'Disco 2000'. Could their profile get any higher?

The answer was an unexpected but unequivocal yes. After tours of Japan and Europe, followed by their biggest ever tour of the UK, including shows at Wembley and the NEC, it might have been reasonable to expect a slightly lower profile for Pulp at the start of 1996. That was before Jarvis (and former Pulp member Pete Mansell) stood up on stage during Michael Jackson's farcical Brit Awards performance, danced oddly, pointed at his buttocks, lobbed the V's and ran off, returning to his seat to laugh with the rest of the band. The good humour soon stopped when he was arrested and threatened with charges of actual bodily harm to three child performers. The award ceremony was the most contentious since the great Sam Fox/Mick Fleetwood debacle, with Jackson taking to the stage after an unusually fawning introduction from the normally astute Bob Geldof.

Jackson's contract stipulated that he be referred to as The King Of Pop, that he could show a film promoting himself prior to his performance and that he had editorial control in the cutting room before the event was broadcast the following night. The snivelling Brit authorities even invented an award for him, the 'Jacko's Great Cos Jacko Says So Award'. His rendition of the tiresome 'Earth Song' was bad enough, but when he stripped to white undergarments and was caressed by children, and then assumed a Christ-like pose and blessed a rabbi in clear self-deification, Jarvis had had enough. He stormed the stage as a protest.

For his troubles he spent three hours in a dressing room being questioned by police, whilst *Men Behaving Badly* stars Neil Morrissey and Martin Clunes, er, behaved badly and chanted "Free Jarvis" outside. Then he was dragged to the South Kensington station where he was questioned further until he was finally released on bail at 3am. Then, when he awoke the following morning, he found himself on the front page of every tabloid, leading every news story and even making it on to prime time American news as a child beater. Jackson issued a statement saying he was "sickened, saddened, shocked, upset, cheated, angry".

The tide was set to turn, however. It very quickly became clear that Jarvis could no more attack children than Michael Jackson could laugh at himself. With the notable exception of the representatives from Sony, Jackson's record company, virtually the entire music industry, including the erudite Brian Eno, came out in full support of Jarvis. The whole incident was an utter sham and everyone knew it. The normally hostile tabloids now ran 'Justice For Jarvis' campaigns. Unedited video footage of the entire incident exonerated Jarvis and left Sony and Jackson in acute embarrassment. Jarvis stood by his actions, saying in a public statement: "The music industry allows him to indulge his fantasies because of his wealth and power. People go along with it even though they know it is a bit sick. I just couldn't go along with it any more."

It seems that Jarvis struck a chord. There are even rumours, albeit unsubstantiated, of Jackson making a full but private apology to Jarvis. The multi-millionaire King of Pop on bended knee to a man in crimplene trousers and corduroy zipper cardigan from Oxfam. Now that would be something to see. Oh, lest we forget, 'Different Class' got four Brit nominations.

Jarvis was bailed to appear at Kensington Police station on March 11, and when the date arrived there were rival camps of Pulp and Jacko fans outside, shouting abuse at each other. One 16-year-old Jacko supporter was even arrested for obscene language and threatening behaviour. Inside the station, things were considerably more subdued, and Jarvis, as widely expected, saw all charges dropped with speculation that Jacko's lawyers had admitted there were never any to face in the first place. Jarvis said afterwards he was considering "civil-remedies" and more light-heartedly went on to say to a packed press conference: "I don't know Michael but I wish him well and hope he sorts his problems out. I think it's unlikely we'll meet but dancing lessons would be great."

It would be difficult for Pulp to have a higher profile than the one they currently enjoy in Britain. Maybe it wouldn't be such a bad thing to retreat for a while, lie low and take a breather. Highly ironic, considering they strove for over a decade to get there in the first place. They have since donated a track, 'Mile End' to 1996's classic film *Trainspotting*, and Jarvis has worked with Mikki from Lush for the track 'Ciao!' on that band's new album. In addition, Jarvis is working on music for Damien Hirst's new film project, and is considering working with Shaun Ryder of Black Grape. With Jarvis expressing ambitions in the film industry, and with Pulp's own long form video due out soon, to complement the new March single, 'Something Changed', 1996 could see Pulp pursue avenues more akin to their performance art past. Whatever they do, Pulp have already made their mark on British pop in more ways than one. And it only took them fourteen years to do it.

PULP DISCOGRAPHY

Singles

**My Lighthouse (Remix)/
Looking For Life**
Red Rhino RED 32 (7")
May 1983

**Everybody's Problem/
There Was**
Red Rhino RED 37 (7")
September 1983

**Little Girl (With Blue
Eyes)/Simultaneous/Blue
Glow/The Will To Power**
Fire FIRE 5 (12")
December 1985

**Dogs Are Everywhere/
The Mark Of The Devil/
97 Lovers/Aborigine/
Goodnight**
Fire BLAZE 10 (12")
June 1986

**They Suffocate At Night
(Edited Version)/Tunnel
(Cut-Up Version)**
Fire BLAZE 17 (7")
January 1987

**They Suffocate At Night
(Uncut Version)/Tunnel
(Full Length Version)**
Fire BLAZE 17T (12")
January 1987

**Master Of The Universe
(Sanitised Version)/
Manon/Silence**
Fire BLAZE 21T (12")
March 1987

**My Legendary Girlfriend/
Is This House?/
This House Is Condemned**
Fire BLAZE 44T (12")
September 1990

**Countdown/Death Goes
To The Disco/Countdown
(Radio Edit)**
Fire BLAZE 51T (12")
August 1991

**Countdown/Death
Goes To The Disco/
Countdown (Radio Edit)**
Fire BLAZE 51 CD (CD)
August 1991

**O.U. (Gone Gone)/
Space/O.U. (Gone Gone)
(Radio Edit)**
Gift GIF 1 (12")
June 1992

**O.U. (Gone Gone)
(Radio Edit)/SPACE/O.U.
(Gone Gone)**
Gift GIF 1CD (CD)
June 1992

**My Legendary
Girlfriend/Sickly Grin/
Back In L.A.**
Caff CAFF 17
(picture sleeve with insert
in bag, 500 only)
August 1992

**Babies/Styloroc
(Nites Of Suburbia)/
Sheffield: Sex City**
Gift GIF 3 (12")
October 1992

**Babies/Styloroc
(Nites Of Suburbia)/
Sheffield: Sex City/
Sheffield: Sex City
(Instrumental)**
Gift GIF 3CD (CD)
October 1992

**Razzmatazz/Inside
Susan (Abridged Version)**
Gift 7 GIF 6 (7")
February 1993

**Razzmatazz/
Inside Susan: A Story In
3 Songs (Stacks/Inside
Susan/59 Lyndhurst Grove)**

Gift GIF 6 (12")
February 1993

**Razzmatazz/Inside
Susan: A Story In 3 Songs
(Stacks/Inside Susan/
59 Lyndhurst Grove)**
Gift GIF 6 CD (CD)
February 1993

Lipgloss/You're A Nightmare
Island IS 567 (7")
November 1993

**Lipgloss/Deep Fried In
Kelvin/You're A Nightmare**
Island 12IS 567 (12")
November 1993

**Lipgloss/Deep Fried In
Kelvin/You're A Nightmare**
Island CID 567 (CD)
November 1993

**Do You Remember The
First Time?/Street Lites**
Island IS 574 (7")
March 1994

**Do You Remember The
First Time?/Street Lites/
The Babysitter**
Island 12IS 574 (12")
March 1994

**Do You Remember The
First Time?/Street Lites**
Island CIS 574 (cassette, 3/94)
March 1994

**Do You Remember The
First Time?/Street Lites/
The Babysitter**
Island CID 574 (CD)
March 1994

**The Sisters EP
(Babies/Your Sister's
Clothes/Seconds/
His'N'Hers)**
Island IS 595
(7", numbered gatefold
picture sleeve, 33rpm)
May 1994

**The Sisters EP
(Babies/Your Sister's
Clothes/Seconds/
His'N'Hers)**
Island 12IS 595
(12" with art print, stickered
picture sleeve)
May 1994

**The Sisters EP
(Babies/Your Sister's
Clothes/Seconds/
His'N'Hers)**
Island CIS 595 (cassette)
May 1994

The Sisters EP
(Babies/Your Sister's
Clothes/Seconds/
His'N'Hers)
Island CID 595 (CD)
May 1994

Common People/
Underwear/**Common People**
(7" edit)
Island CID613 (CD) 613
May 1995

Common People
(Full Version)/Underwear
Island CIDT613 (CD) 613
May 1995

Common People (Full
Version)/Razzmatazz
(Acoustic Version)/
Dogs Are Everywhere
(Acoustic Version)/
Joyriders (Acoustic Version)
Island CIDX613 (CD)
May 1995

Common People (Motiv8
Vocal Mix)/**Common
People** (Vocoda Mix)/**Common
People** (Full Length
Version)/**Common People**
(7" edit)
Island 12IS613 (12")
May 1995

Common People
(Full Length Version)/
Underwear/**Common People**
(7" edit)
Island 8543294 (cassette)
May 1995

Mis-Shapes/Sorted For
E's And Wizz
Island CID DJ620 (CD)
October 1995

Mis-Shapes/Sorted For
E's And Wizz/P.T.A. (Parent
Teachers Association)
Island CID620 (CD)
October 1995

Mis-Shapes/Sorted For
E's And Wizz/**Common
People** (Motiv8 Club Mix)
Island CIDZ620 (CD)
October 1995

**Sorted For E's And
Wizz**/Mis-Shapes/**Common
People** (Motiv8 Club
Mix)/**Common People**
(Vocoda Mix)
Island CIDX620 (CD)
October 1995

Mis-Shapes/Sorted For
E's And Wizz
Island CIDT620 (CD)
October 1995

Mis-Shapes/Sorted For
E's And Wizz
Island ISJB620 (7")
October 1995

Mis-Shapes/Sorted For
E's And Wizz
Island CIS620 (cassette)
October 1995

Disco 2000/Disco 2000
(7" Mix)/Disco 2000 (Motiv8
Discoid Mix)/Disco 2000
(Motiv8 Gimp Mix)
Island CIDX 623 (CD)
November 1995

Disco 2000 (7" Mix)/Disco
2000 (Motiv8 Discoid Mix)
Island CIDT 623 (CD)
November 1995

Disco 2000 (7" Mix)/Disco
2000 (Motiv8 Discoid Mix)
Island ISJB 623
(7" juke box single)
November 1995

Disco 2000 (7" Mix)/Disco
2000 (Motiv8 Discoid Mix)
Island CIS 623 (cassette)
November 1995

Something Changed/
Mile End/F.E.E.L.I.N.G.S.
C.A.L.L.E.D.L.O.V.E.
(The Moloko Mix)/
F.E.E.L.I.N.G.S.C.A.L.L.E.D.
L.O.V.E.
Island CID 632
(CD, picture of girl on sleeve)
March 1996

Something Changed/
Mile End/F.E.E.L.I.N.G.S.
C.A.L.L.E.D.L.O.V.E.
(The Moloko Mix)/
F.E.E.L.I.N.G.S.C.A.L.L.E.D.
L.O.V.E.
Island CIDX632
(CD, picture of boy on sleeve)
March 1996

Something Changed/
Mile End
Island (CD) CIDT632
March 1996

Something Changed/
Disco 2000 (7" Mix)
Island ISJB632
(7", Jukebox only)
March 1996

Something Changed/
Mile End
Island CIS632 (cassette)
March 1996

CDs

Separations
Love Is Blind/Don't You
Want Me Anymore/
She's Dead/Separations/
Down By The River/
Countdown/My Legendary
Girlfriend/Death II/
This House Is Condemned
Fire FIRE 33026
July 1992

Freaks
Fairgirl/I Want You/Being
Followed Home/Master
Of The Universe/Life Must
Be So Wonderful/There's
No Emotion/Anorexic
Beauty/The Never Ending
Story/Don't You Know/
They Suffocate At Night
Fire FIRE CD5
July 1993

**Pulpintro –
The Gift Recordings**
Space/O.U. (Gone Gone)/
Babies/Stylorock (Nights Of
Suburbia)/Razzmatazz/
Sheffield: Sex City/Inside
Susan: A Story In Three Songs
(Stacks/Inside Susan/
59, Lindhurst Grove)
Island IMCD 159
(mid-price; also on cassette)
October 1993

It
(See LPs for track listing)
Cherry Red CDMRED 112
(reissue with extra tracks
'Everybody's Problem',
'There Was' & 'Looking For
Life', withdrawn, 1,000 only)
February 1994

His'N'Hers
Joy Rider/Lipgloss/
Acrylic Afternoons/Have
You Seen Her Lately/She's
A Lady/Happy Ending/
Do You Remember The First
Time?/Pink Glove/Someone
Like The Moon/David's
Last Summer/
Island CID 8025
April 1994

**Masters Of The Universe –
Pulp On Fire 1985-86**
Little Girl/Simultaneous/
Blue Glow/The Will To
Power/Dogs Are Everywhere/
The Mask Of The Devil/
97 Lovers/Aborigine/
Goodnight/They Suffocate At
Night/Tunnel/Master Of The
Universe (Sanitised Version)/
Manon/They Suffocate
At Night
Fire FIRE CD36
June 1994

It
(See LPs for track listing)
Fire REFIRE CD15
(2nd reissue, with extra track
'Looking For Life')
November 1994

Different Class
Mis-shapes/Pencil Skirt/
Common People/I Spy/
Disco 2000/Live Bed Show/
Something Changed/Sorted For
E's & Wizz/F.E.E.L.I.N.G.
C.A.L.L.E.D.L.O.V.E./
Underwear/Monday
Morning/Bar Italia
Island CID8041
November 1995

Countdown
Countdown (Radio Edit)/
Death Goes To The Disco/
My Legendary Girlfriend/
Don't You Want Me Anymore/
She's Dead/Down By The
River/I Want You/Being
Followed Home/Master Of
The Universe/Don't You Know

LPs

It
My Lighthouse/Wishful
Thinking/Joking Aside/Boats
And Trains/Blue Girls/
Love Love/In Many Ways/
Looking For Life/Everybody's
Problem/There Was
Red Rhino REDLP 29
(Mini-LP)
April 1983

Freaks
(See CD for track listing)
Fire FIRE LP5
May 1987

Separations
(See CD for track listing)
Fire FIRE 11025
July 1992

**Pulpintro – The Gift
Recordings**
(See CD for track listing)
Island ILPM 2076 (mid-price)
October 1993

His'N'Hers
(See CD for track listing
with extra track 'Babies' on LP;
also on cassette)
Island ILPS 8025
April 1994

**Masters Of The Universe –
Pulp On Fire 1985-86**
(See CD for track listing)
Fire FIRE LP36 (compilation)
June 1994

Miscellaneous Compilations Featuring Pulp Tracks

Your Secret's Safe With Us
Statik STATLP 7 (2-LP, includes
'What Do You Say?') 1982

**The Best Of Your Secret's
Safe With Us**
Statik STATLP 14 (LP, single
disc compilation of above,
includes 'What Do You Say?')
1983

Company Classics No. 3
Company Classics (cassette,
includes demos of 'Coy
Mistress' & 'I Want You') 1985

Beware The Bacon Slicer
Pork CUISINE 2 (cassette,
includes demos of 'Coy
Mistress' & 'Anorexic Beauty')
April 1986

Imminent Vol. 4
Food BITE 4 (includes
different mix of 'Manon')
August 1986

Premonition Art Construct
Premonition PREM 5
(cassette, includes 'Back
In LA' demo)
1986

Premspeak 1
Premonition (cassette
magazine, includes demo of
'Maureen' & interview with
Jarvis & Russell)
1986

See You Later Agitator
Doublebusters (cassette
in 7" sleeve, includes live
version of 'Nights Of Suburbia')
1986

**Oozing Through The
Ozone Layer**
Globe Of Bulbs LSD 5
(cassette, includes live
versions of 'My First Wife' &
'Don't You Want Me
Anymore?')
September 1987

Volume Ten
Volume 10VCD10
(CD book, includes acoustic
version of 'Joyriders')
1994

The Radio 1 FM Sessions
Vox GIVIT 8 (cassette
free with Vox, includes live
version of 'Do You Remember
The First Time?' at Glasgow
Sound City)
September 1994